MACHINE

LEARNING

WITH

PYTHON

*A Step-By-Step Guide to Learn and
Master Python Machine Learning*

HEIN SMITH

TABLE OF CONTENTS

Introduction

Do you want to learn how to do machine learning with Python but you have problems getting started? In this book, you'll learn all the important topics that you need to know for you to implement machine learning with Python. You'll learn how to download, install Python, and get the best package for machine learning in Python. You'll also load a dataset and understand its structure using data visualization and summaries. If you are new to machine learning and looking to eventually launch a career in Python, this book was designed for you.

Python is a powerful interpreted language. Unlike other languages such as R, Python is a complete language and platform where you can apply both research and development production. Still, there are many modules and libraries which you can select from and generate different ways to perform each task.

Methods in machine learning are popularly used in a wide variety of fields such as engineering, sciences, physics, and computer systems. Additionally, it is also used by commercial websites for the recommendation system, advertising, and predicting the actions of a customer.

Machine Learning has popped out as a major engine of most commercial applications and research endeavors. But this particular branch does not exclude large research companies. In this book, you'll get an in-depth introduction to the field of machine learning from linear models to deep learning and reinforcement learning. You will understand the principles behind machine learning problems like regression, reinforcement learning, and classification.

Chapter 1

Python Basics

Welcome! Is this your first time to programming? If not, then we assume that you want to learn how to use machine learning with python. Also, you could be looking for information about why and how you can get started with Python. If you are an expert programmer in any language, it will be easy for you to pick up Python very fast.

Before you can get started in Python, you need to know how to install Python on your computer. Next, you need to know a few concepts about the language syntax to be able to read and understand the python code. This chapter will take you through all these. So, get ready to learn a few important things in Python language.

Installing
Nowadays, most UNIX and Linux distributions already come with a recent Python version installed. Even some HP Microsoft computers have Python already installed.

Download Python
Before you can get started with Machine Learning with Python, you must have Python installed on your computer, however, you might not need to download it.

So, the first thing to do is to confirm that Python is not installed by typing "Python" in a command window. When you see a response from a Python interpreter, it will consist of a version number in its original display. In general, any recent version will work because Python tries to maintain backward compatibility.

If you want to install Python, you might as well search for the most recent stable version. This version will have the highest number not marked as an alpha or beta release.

If you're running a Windows OS, the most stable Windows' downloads can be found from the Python for Windows page.

If you're running Windows XP, you'll find a complete guide to installing ActivePython at "Python on XP".

For those using a Mac, you can navigate to "Python for Mac OS X page."

For those using Debian or Ubuntu, you should install python2x and pythonn2.x-deve packages.

Syntax

Python programs are written with the help of a text editor and must have an extension .py. It is not a must to have the first and last line in Python programs but it can assign the location of python as the first line **#!/usr/bin/python** and become executable. Nonetheless, the command prompt is another environment from which you can run python programs by entering "python file.py". In Python, there are no semicolons and braces. It is a high-level language. So instead of braces, blocks are selected by selecting the same indentation.

First Python program

Usually, when you start to learn any programming language, your first program to write will be "Hello, World!". This is an easy program that prints "Hello, World!" For our first python program, you will learn how to write a program which adds two numbers.

A program that adds two numbers

```
# Add two numbers
num1 = 3
num2 = 5
sum = num1+num2
print(sum)
```

How does the above program work?

The first line of the program begins with a comment. Comments in python programming are written starting with #. Python interpreter and compilers ignore comments. The reason why comments should be applied in Python programming is to describe the function of the code. Furthermore, comments help any other programmer to understand the working of your code.

Variables and Datatypes

A data type, as the name suggests, is the category of data in different types. It defines a collection of values plus operations that can take place on those values. The explicit value used in our programs is a literal. For instance, 11, 30.22, 'pypi' are all literals. Each literal has a type linked to it. For example, 11 is an int type, 30.22 is a float type and 'pypi' is of type string. Often, the type of literal will determine the type of operations that can be done to it. The table below contains basic data types in Python.

Types of data	In Python we call them	Examples
Integers	int	12, -999, 0, 900000, etc
Real Numbers	float	4.5, 0.0003, -90.5, 3.0; etc
Characters	str	'hello', "100", "$$$", ""; etc

Python contains an inbuilt function called type () which is used to define the data type of the literal.

```
>>>
>>> type(54)
<class 'int'>
>>>
>>> type("a string")
<class 'str'>
>>>
>>> type(98.188)
<class 'float'>
>>>
>>> type("3.14")
<class 'str'>
>>>
>>> type("99")
<class 'str'>
>>>
```

The <class 'int'> describes that the type of 54 is int. Also, <class 'str'> and <class 'float'> shows that "a string" and 98. 188 is of type str and float respectively.

At first, you might say that "3.14" is of type float but since it is wrapped inside double quotes, it is definitely a string. In the same way, "99" is a string.

A sequence of character data is a string. The string type in Python is called str.

String literals can either be defined by single or double quotes. All the characters inside the opening and closing quotes are part of the string as shown below:

```
>>> "

"
```

Escape sequence in strings

There are times when you want Python to interpret a sequence of characters inside a string differently. This might happen in one or two ways:

• If you want to suppress the unique interpretation that specific characters are supplied within a string.

• You want to apply specific interpretation to characters contained in a string that is often taken literally.

You can do this by using the backslash (\) character. A backslash character in a string implies that one or more characters which follow it must be uniquely treated. This is called an escape sequence because the backslash will make subsequent character sequence to "escape" its normal meaning.

Boolean Type

Python 3 has a Boolean data type. Objects of Boolean type may contain one or two values, False or True.

```
>>> type(True)
<class 'bool'>
>>> type(False)
<class 'bool'>
```

Python expressions are evaluated in a Boolean context. This means that they are interpreted to represent false or truth. A true value in Boolean is described as "Truthy" while a false value is described as "Falsy."

The truthiness of an object of the Boolean type is open. This means that objects which are equal to True are Truthy, and those that are equal to False are Falsy. However, objects that are not of Boolean type can be evaluated in a Boolean context and determined to be true or false.

Python Variables

In the first Python program, you were introduced to Python variables. You briefly saw how you can define variables in Python and assign them some values. This section discusses more variables in Python.

Variables like in any other programming languages are used to store values. Also, you can use variables to access data and manipulate data.

Create a variable

If you want to create a variable in Python, you must use the assignment operator. The format shown below is applied when you want to create a variable.

```
variable_name = expression
```

An example can include:

    number = 12.

This statement will create a variable called number and assign it the value 12. When the Python interpreter comes across this statement, it performs the following things behind the scenes.

1. Store the variable "12" in a given location in memory.

2. Make the variable number point to it.

The crucial thing to understand is that the variable number itself doesn't have any value, it only points to the memory location that contains the original value.

Another important thing to note is that when you assign a value to a variable, make sure that you write the variable name on the left side of the assignment (=) operator. If you fail to do this, you will get a syntax error.

Python always detects the type of variable and operations performed on it depending on the value it has. The programming jargon that describes this is called, Dynamic Typing. This means that you can use the same variable to refer to a different type of data that initially points to.

Any time you assign a new value to a variable, the reference to the previous value is lost. For instance, if the variable number is assigned the string "ten", the reference to value "12" is lost. At this point, there will be no variable that will point to the memory location. When this takes place, the Python interpreter will automatically remove the value from the memory through garbage collection.

If you try to access a variable before you assign a value to it, you will get a NameError.

Control Flow

The control flow in a program highlights the order of program execution. In a Python program, control flow is carried out by function calls, conditional statements, and loops. This section will deal with the If Statement, While and For loops.

If Statement

There are occasions which you may want to run certain statements if some condition holds, or decide the type of statements to run based on different mutually exclusive conditions. Python has the compound "If Statement" that is made up of "if", "elif", and "else" clauses. These compound statements allow you to conditionally create blocks of statements. Below is a general declaration of an If Statement.

```
if expression:
    statement(s)
elif expression:
    statement(s)
elif expression:
    statement(s)
...
else:
    statement(s)
```

Here, "elif "and "else" clause are optional. As a reminder, there are no switch statements in Python, this means that you need to apply "elif", "if", and "else" for conditional processing. Take a look at this example of an If program.

```
if x < 0: print "x is negative"
elif x % 2: print "x is positive and odd"
else: print "x is even and non-negative"
```

The While statement

In Python, a WHILE statement supports the repeated execution of a statement or even a block of statement which are under the control of a conditional expression. Take a look of a While syntax.

```
while expression:
    statement(s)
```

A While statement can also consist of an 'else' clause, 'break and continue' statements. Below is an example of a While program example in Python.

```
count = 0
while x > 0:
    x = x // 2                  # truncating division
    count += 1
print "The approximate log2 is", count
```

The for Statement

The Python language also contains the for statement which supports repeated program statement execution. The for statement has an iterable expression to control the blocks of statements. Below is a general syntax of a for statement.

```
for target in iterable:
    statement(s)
```

Keep in mind that "in" is a keyword. It is part of the syntax of the For Statement but not associated with the "in" operator which is applied in the membership testing. A for Statement can have an else clause, break, and continue statements. Here is a general declaration form of a For Statement:

```
for letter in "ciao":
    print "give me a", letter, "..."
```

Data Structures

They are structures which assist in data storage. Data structures have a collection of data linked to each other. In Python, there are 4 built-in data structures. They are as follows:

- Tuple

- List

- Dictionary

- Set

Below is a detail description of each data structure.

List

A list describes data structures which have an ordered set of items. Consider a shopping list that has several items which you need to purchase. The only difference is that your shopping list has each item on a separate line.

However, in the case of a list in Python, you only need to separate your items with commas. The moment you create a list, you have the permission to add, remove, or search items in the same list. Since a list allows you to add and remove items, it is considered as a mutable data type. This means that you can change it anytime.

Quick Intro to Objects and Classes

To understand more about a list in Python language, it is good to quickly introduce you to the concept of objects and classes. A list is an example of objects and classes. So, if you are going to use a variable such as j and allocate it a value say integer 7, then it is important to look at it as if you are creating object j.

A class contains methods. Methods and functions are similar. However, methods are defined inside that class alone. Therefore, the only way to access a function is by having an object in that class. For example, in the Python language, you can join a method to a list class that allows the class of the object.

The Python language has the append method for a list class which permits the addition of an item to the end of the list. Classes in Python have fields which take the form of variables declared to be used in a specific class alone. This means that if you want to use these variables, you require to have an object of that class alone. You access fields with the help of a dotted notation. For example, mylist.field.

```python
# This is my shopping list
shoplist = ['apple', 'mango', 'carrot', 'banana']

print('I have', len(shoplist), 'items to purchase.')

print('These items are:', end=' ')
for item in shoplist:
    print(item, end=' ')

print('\nI also have to buy rice.')
shoplist.append('rice')
print('My shopping list is now', shoplist)
print('I will sort my list now')
shoplist.sort()
print('Sorted shopping list is', shoplist)

print('The first item I will buy is', shoplist[0])
olditem = shoplist[0]
del shoplist[0]
print('I bought the', olditem)
print('My shopping list is now', shoplist)
```

Output:

```
$ python ds_using_list.py
I have 4 items to purchase.
These items are: apple mango carrot banana
I also have to buy rice.
My shopping list is now ['apple', 'mango', 'carrot', 'banana', 'rice']
I will sort my list now
Sorted shopping list is ['apple', 'banana', 'carrot', 'mango', 'rice']
The first item I will buy is apple
I bought the apple
My shopping list is now ['banana', 'carrot', 'mango', 'rice']
```

Here's how it works

There is the variable, "shoplist" which has information about a person planning to go to the market. The "shoplist" allows you to store strings of names of things which you plan to buy. However, you can add any type of object like numbers.

This program also has a 'for' loop which will support iteration in the list. You should have started to realize that a list is similar to a sequence. Notice how the end parameters are used to call a print function. This shows that you want to end the output with space rather than a normal line break.

Next, you should add an item to the list using the append method. Check whether the item is added using the print function.

There is also a sorting method in the program. The purpose of this is to sort the list. It is important to note that this particular method affects the list itself and it can't return an altered list.

The next thing is to complete purchasing the item from the market. This process is equivalent to removing an item from the list. You do this with the help of the del Statement. For this scenario, you need to describe the item found in the list which you want to remove. Then use the del Statement to remove it from the list.

After that, the del Statement removes it from the list. To remove an item in a list using Python, you just write the following line function del shoplist [0].

Tuple

Tuples store multiple objects. They are similar to lists except that they don't have a lot of functions like a list class. One great feature about tuples is that it is immutable like strings. This implies that it is hard to change the tuples.

If you want to define tuples, you have to describe items and separate them with commas. Tuples are best used in cases where the collection of values can't change. Take for example:

```
# I would recommend always using parentheses
# to indicate start and end of tuple
# even though parentheses are optional.
# Explicit is better than implicit.
zoo = ('python', 'elephant', 'penguin')
print('Number of animals in the zoo is', len(zoo))
new_zoo = 'monkey', 'camel', zoo
print('Number of cages in the new zoo is', len(new_zoo))
print('All animals in new zoo are', new_zoo)
print('Animals brought from old zoo are', new_zoo[2])
print('Last animal brought from old zoo is', new_zoo[2][2])
print('Number of animals in the new zoo is',
     len(new_zoo)-1+len(new_zoo[2]))
```

```
Output:

$ python ds_using_tuple.py
Number of animals in the zoo is 3
Number of cages in the new zoo is 3
All animals in new zoo are ('monkey', 'camel', ('python', 'elephant', 'penguin'))
Animals brought from old zoo are ('python', 'elephant', 'penguin')
Last animal brought from old zoo is penguin
Number of animals in the new zoo is 5
```

Dictionaries

A dictionary is similar to an address book which you can search details of a person by selecting his or her name. In a dictionary, keys are joined with values. Keep in mind that the key must be unique and you can again use immutable objects for dictionary keys by either applying mutable or immutable objects for the dictionary values. Remember that the key-value pairs in the dictionary don't have a fixed arrangement.

Example:

```
# 'ab' is short for 'a'ddress'b'ook

ab = {
    'Swaroop': 'swaroop@swaroopch.com',
    'Larry': 'larry@wall.org',
    'Matsumoto': 'matz@ruby-lang.org',
    'Spammer': 'spammer@hotmail.com'
}

print("Swaroop's address is", ab['Swaroop'])

# Deleting a key-value pair
del ab['Spammer']

print('\nThere are {} contacts in the address-book\n'.format(len(ab)))

for name, address in ab.items():
    print('Contact {} at {}'.format(name, address))

# Adding a key-value pair
ab['Guido'] = 'guido@python.org'

if 'Guido' in ab:
    print("\nGuido's address is", ab['Guido'])
```

```
Output:

$ python ds_using_dict.py
Swaroop's address is swaroop@swaroopch.com

There are 3 contacts in the address-book

Contact Swaroop at swaroop@swaroopch.com
Contact Matsumoto at matz@ruby-lang.org
Contact Larry at larry@wall.org

Guido's address is guido@python.org
```

```python
x = 50


def func():
    global x

    print('x is', x)
    x = 2
    print('Changed global x to', x)


func()
print('Value of x is', x)
```

Chapter 2

Introduction to Machine Learning

The focus of Machine Learning is to learn the nature of data and apply it to specific models.

Although ML is a field in computer science, it is not the same as the traditional computational methods. When you look at traditional computing, algorithms are described as a set of programmed instructions. These instructions provide solutions to a problem.

ML algorithms make computers to learn from data inputs and apply statistical analysis to display values found in a given range. Therefore, ML allows computers to create a model from a data sample so that it can permit the automation of decisions based on the type of data entered.

Nowadays, technology users hugely benefit from the idea of machine learning. For example, the facial recognition technology provides opportunities to social media networks so that their users can tag and share photos with their friends.

There is also the optical character recognition (OCR). This type of technology is applied in movies, shows, and e-commerce to suggest to users based on their preferences. If you know self–driving cars, they also depend on machine learning to move.

This chapter will take you through some of the most common ML methods of supervised and unsupervised learning, as well as popular machine learning algorithms. Additionally, you'll learn why you need machine learning and some of the programming languages used with machine learning besides Python. Furthermore, this chapter will also look at some of the biases associated with machine learning, and consider a few things to help reduce these types of biases when you build an algorithm.

Machine Learning Methods

When it comes to the field of machine learning, there are tasks which are categorized into different divisions. Most of these divisions depend on how learning is performed, or on the type of feedback delivered based on the system developed.

The most popular machine learning methods include supervised learning and unsupervised learning. For supervised learning, algorithms learn from the example of input and output data labeled by humans. On the other hand, unsupervised learning does not supply to the algorithm any labeled data, but the algorithm has to find the structure within its input data by itself. Here's a detail discussion of these methods.

Supervised Learning

For supervised learning, the computer has an example of input data to work on. The aim of this method is to allow the algorithm to "learn" by comparing actual output using a trained output to discover errors and alter the model. In other words, this method contains patterns which assist in predicting label values on extra data that is unlabeled.

For example, in supervised learning, you can feed an algorithm data with shark images and label them as fish. Also, you can feed it with images of oceans and label it like water.

After the algorithm is trained several times with this particular data, the algorithm must be able to differentiate unlabeled fish images and unlabeled ocean images.

One of the most popular use cases of supervised learning is the application of historical data to help forecast the statistical chance of an event to happen. It can use historical stock market data to predict future changes in the market. Additionally, supervised learning can help in the filtering of spam emails. Supervised learning makes it possible to classify untagged photos of dogs by using photos of dogs that have been tagged already.

Unsupervised learning

Unlike supervised learning where data is labeled, with unsupervised learning, you deal with unlabeled data. This means that it is the task of the learning algorithm to identify similar features in the data that it is supplied. Since unlabeled data is very popular compared to labeled data, techniques of machine learning are among the most valuable in the industry. The aim of unsupervised learning is very simple.

The largest application of unsupervised learning is within the transactional data. There can be a massive data set made up of customers and the products which they purchase, but since you are a human, you can't manage to extract meaning and similarity from customer profile and their purchase history.

The best time to apply unsupervised machine learning is when you don't have data on expected outcomes, like defining a target market for a new product that your business has never sold before, but if you are attempting to understand your consumer base, supervised learning is the right technique.

Machine learning approaches

Machine learning is highly linked to computational statistics. For that reason, if you have some knowledge of statistics, it is important to understand and apply machine learning algorithms.

If you are new to statistics, here are some definition of terms which are popularly used in detecting the relation found in quantitative variables.

Correlation. This describes the association that exists between two variables said not to be independent or dependent.

Regression. At the lowest level, it is helpful at determining the relationship between one independent and dependent variable.

The k-nearest neighbor

This particular algorithm is applied in the pattern recognition model. Pattern recognition model is used in classification and regression. The k is a positive integer. In both regression and classification, the input contains k closest training example in a specific space.

The KNN classification

When it comes to this method, its output belongs to the class membership. This assigns a new object the most popular class in the k-nearest neighbors. Take for example, when k = 1, the object has to be assigned a class which has one nearest neighbor. The diagram below describes this algorithm. The diagram has blue diamond objects and orange star objects. Just remember that they belong to two different classes. That is the star and diamond classes.

Once you introduce a new object to space such as a green heart, you'll need the learning algorithm to assign the heart into a particular class.

For k = 3, the algorithm will have to pick three nearest neighbors that belong to the green heart and assign it, either into the diamond or star class.

In this case, the three nearest neighbors of the green heart consist of the diamond and two stars. Therefore, the algorithm can label the heart that contains the star class.

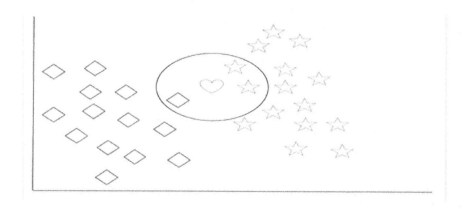

The k-nearest neighbor algorithm is among the basic machine learning algorithms labeled as "Lazy learning".

Decision Tree

In general, decision trees are important when you want to have a visual representation of decisions and display decision making. When working with ML and data mining, decision trees are key when it comes to a predictive model. The model contains observations and creates a summary related to the target value of the data.

Learning in decision trees is important when you want to create a model that is useful at predicting a value depending on the input values.

If you take a look at a predictive model, the features of the data have to be defined using observation and represented by branches. Additionally, conclusions related to the data's target value are shown in the leaves.

This example demonstrates the various conditions that can show whether a person is supposed to go fishing or not.

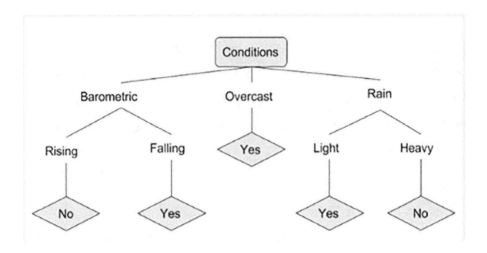

This decision tree is classified by sorting. Then it can display which classification is associated with a particular leaf. In the following example, it is a yes or no. The tree can then divide the day's condition based on whether it is correct to go fishing or not.

A real classification tree dataset will contain a lot more features compared to what is shown in this tree. All in all, 'relationship' will be easy to select.

Deep Learning
With deep learning, it will always try to copy the human brain and how it succeeds in processing sound and light stimuli. The underlining architecture of deep learning is powered by biological neural networks. Additionally, it contains many different multiple layers.

In the current machine learning algorithms, deep learning has succeeded in selecting most of the data as well as defeat humans in different cognitive tasks. Due to the following properties, deep learning is one of the best methods applied in AI.

Programming Languages

When a person wants to choose a language to use to learn with machine learning, there are few things that they may want to factor in such as the current status of job positions and the type of libraries available. Other languages that are used in machine language include C++, Java, and R.

Human Biases

While both data and computational analysis cause an individual to start to think like they aren't being objective, being biased on a given data doesn't mean that the output from the machine learning is neutral. The human bias affects the organization of data and algorithms that determine how ML should use data.

If you decide to use historical photographs of scientists in your specific computer training, a computer might fail to classify scientists.

Although machine learning is continuously applied in the business, biases that go unnoticed can lead to a systematic problem that can prevent people from receiving loans and many other things.

In short, human biases can negatively impact other people. This is very important to underline and work towards removing it as possible. One particular method which you can use to achieve zero biases is to ensure that several people work on a project. Since machine learning is an area which is continuously being improved, it is essential to remember that algorithms, approaches, and methods continue to change.

Chapter 3

Data Processing, Analysis, and Visualization

Understanding Data Processing

Data processing is the act of changing the nature of data into a form that is more useful and desirable. In other words, it is making data more meaningful and informative. By applying machine learning algorithms, statistical knowledge, and mathematical modeling, one can automate this whole process. The output of this whole process can be in any form like tables, graphs, charts, images, and much more, based on the activity done and the requirements of the machine.

This might appear simple, but for big organizations and companies like Facebook, Twitter, UNESCO, and health sector organizations, this whole process has to be carried out in a structured way. The diagram below shows some of the steps that are followed:

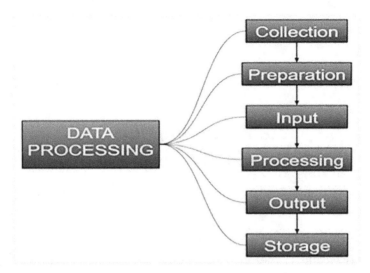

Let's look in detail at each step:

Collection

The most important step when getting started with Machine Learning is to ensure that the data available is of great quality. You can collect data from genuine sources such as Kaggle, data.gov.in, and UCI dataset repository. For example, when students are getting ready to take a competitive exam, they always find the best resources to use to ensure they attain good results. Similarly, accurate and high-quality data will simplify the learning process of the model. This means that during the time of testing, the model would output the best results.

A great amount of time, capital, and resources are involved in data collection. This means that organizations and researchers have to select the correct type of data which they want to implement or research.

For instance, to work on the Facial Expression Recognition requires a lot of images that have different human expressions. A good data will make sure that the results of the model are correct and genuine.

Preparation

The data collected can be in raw form. Raw data cannot be directly fed into a machine. Instead, something has to be done on the data first. The preparation stage involves gathering data from a wide array of sources, analyzing the datasets, and then building a new data set for additional processing and exploration. Preparation can be done manually or automatically and the data should be prepared in a numerical form to improve the rate of learning of the model.

Input

Sometimes, data already prepared can be in the form which the machine cannot read, in this case, it has to be converted into readable form. For conversion to take place, it is important for a specific algorithm to be present.

To execute this task, intensive computation and accuracy are required. For example, you can collect data through sources like MNIST, audio files, twitter comments, and video clips.

Processing

In this stage, ML techniques and algorithms are required to execute instructions generated over a large volume of data with accuracy and better computation.

Output

In this phase, results get procured by the machine in a sensible way such that the user can decide to reference it. Output can appear in the form of videos, graphs, and reports.

Storage

This is the final stage where the generated output, data model, and any other important information are saved for future use.

Data Processing in Python

Let's learn something in python libraries before looking at how you can use Python to process and analyze data. The first thing is to be familiar with some important libraries. You need to know how you can import them into the environment. There are different ways to do this in Python.

You can type:

Import math as m

From math import *

In a first way, you define an alias m to library math. Then you can use different functions from the math library by making a reference using an alias m. factorial ().

In the second method, you import the whole namespace in math. You can choose to directly apply factorial () without inferring to math.

Note:

Google recommends the first method of importing libraries because it will help you tell the origin of the functions.

The list below shows libraries that you'll need to know where the functions originate from.

NumPy: This stands for Numerical Python. The most advanced feature of NumPy is an n-dimensional array. This library has a standard linear algebra function, advanced random number capability, and tools for integration with other low-level programming languages.

SciPy: It is the shorthand for Scientific Python. SciPy is designed on NumPy. It is among the most important library for different high-level science and engineering modules such as Linear Algebra, Sparse matrices, and Fourier transform.

Matplotlib: This is best applied when you have a lot of graphs which you need to plot. It begins from line plots to heat plots and you can apply the Pylab feature in IPython notebook to ensure plotting features are inline.

Pandas: Best applied in structured data operations and manipulations. It is widely used for data preparation and mining. Pandas were introduced recently to Python and have been very useful in enhancing Python's application in the data scientist community.

scikit-learn: This is designed for machine learning. It was created on matplotlib, NumPy, and SciPy. This specific library has a lot of efficient tools for machine learning and statistical modeling. That includes regression, classification, clustering, and dimensionality community.

StatsModels: This library is designed for statistical modeling. Statsmodels refers to a Python module which permits users to explore data, approximate statistical models, and implement statistical tests.

Other libraries

- Requests used to access the web.

- Blaze used to support the functionality of NumPy and Pandas.

- Bokeh used to create dashboards, interactive plots, and data applications on the current web browsers.

- Seaborn is used in statistical data visualization.

- Regular expressions that are useful for discovering patterns in a text data

- NetWorx and Igraph applied to graph data manipulations.

Now that you are familiar with Python fundamentals and crucial libraries, let's now jump into problem-solving through Python.

An exploratory analysis in Python with Pandas

If you didn't know, Pandas is an important data analysis library in Python. This library has been key to improving the application of Python in the data science community. Our example uses Pandas to read a data set from an analytics Vidhya competition, run an exploratory analysis, and create a first categorization algorithm to solve this problem.

Before you can load the data, it is important to know the two major data structures in Pandas. That is Series and DataFrames.

Series and DataFrames

You can think of series as a 1-dimensional labeled array. These labels help you to understand individual elements of this series via labels.

A data frame resembles an Excel workbook and contains column names which refer to columns as well as rows that can be accessed by row numbers. The most important difference is that column names and row numbers are referred to as column and row index.

Series and data frames create a major data model for Pandas in Python. At first, the datasets have to be read from data frames and different operations can easily be subjected to these columns.

Practice data set – Loan Prediction Problem

The following is the description of variables:

```
VARIABLE DESCRIPTIONS:
Variable              Description
Loan_ID               Unique Loan ID
Gender                Male/ Female
Married               Applicant married (Y/N)
Dependents            Number of dependents
Education             Applicant Education (Graduate/ Under Graduat
e)
Self_Employed         Self employed (Y/N)
ApplicantIncome       Applicant income
CoapplicantIncome     Coapplicant income
LoanAmount            Loan amount in thousands
Loan_Amount_Term      Term of loan in months
Credit_History        credit history meets guidelines
Property_Area         Urban/ Semi Urban/ Rural
Loan_Status           Loan approved (Y/N)
```

First, start iPython interface in Inline Pylab mode by typing the command below on the terminal:

```
ipython notebook --pylab=inline
```

Import libraries and data set

This chapter will use the following python libraries:

- NumPy

- Matplotlib

33

- Pandas

Once you have imported the library, you can move on and read the dataset using a function read_csv(). Below is how the code will look till this point.

```
import pandas as pd
import numpy as np
import matplotlib as plt
%matplotlib inline
#Reading the dataset in a dataframe using Pandas
df = pd.read_csv("/home/kunal/Downloads/Loan_Prediction/train.csv")
```

Notice that the dataset is stored in

"/home/kunal/Downloads/Loan_Prediction/train.csv"

Once you read the dataset, you can decide to check a few top rows by using the **function head().**

Next, you can check at the summary of numerical fields by using the **describe () function.**

Distribution analysis

Since you are familiar with the basic features of data, this is the time to look at the distribution of different variables. Let's begin with numeric variables-ApplicantIncome and LoanAmount.

First, type the commands below to plot the histogram of ApplicantIncome.

```
df['ApplicantIncome'].hist(bins=50)
```

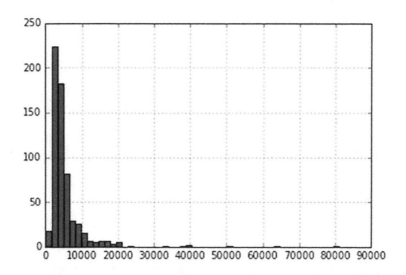

Notice that there are a few extreme values. This is why 50 bins are needed to represent the distribution clearly.

The next thing to focus on is the box plot. The box plot for fare is plotted by:

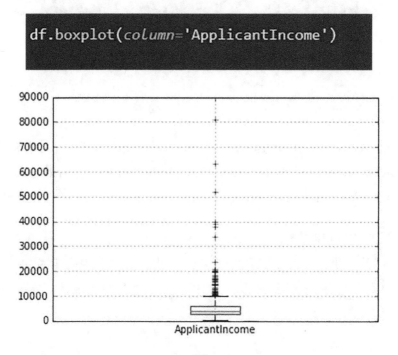

This is just a tip of an iceberg when it comes data processing in Python.

Let's look at:

Techniques for Preprocessing Data in Python

Here are the best techniques for Data Preprocessing in Python.

1. Rescaling Data

When you work with data that has different scales, you need to rescale the properties to have the same scale. The properties are rescaled between the range 0 to 1 and refer to it as normalization. To achieve this, the MinMaxScaler class from scikit-learn is used. For example:

```
>>> import pandas, scipy, numpy
>>> from sklearn.preprocessing import MinMaxScaler
>>> df=pandas.read_csv( 'http://archive.ics.uci.edu/ml/machine-learning-databases/wine-quality/winequality-red.csv ',sep=';')
>>> array=df.values
>>> #Separating data into input and output components
>>> x=array[:,0:8]
>>> y=array[:,8]
>>> scaler=MinMaxScaler(feature_range=(0,1))
>>> rescaledX=scaler.fit_transform(x)
>>> numpy.set_printoptions(precision=3) #Setting precision for the output
>>> rescaledX[0:5,:]
```

```
>>> rescaledX[0:5,:]
array([[0.248, 0.397, 0.   , 0.068, 0.107, 0.141, 0.099, 0.568],
       [0.283, 0.521, 0.   , 0.116, 0.144, 0.338, 0.216, 0.494],
       [0.283, 0.438, 0.04 , 0.096, 0.134, 0.197, 0.17 , 0.509],
       [0.584, 0.11 , 0.56 , 0.068, 0.105, 0.225, 0.191, 0.582],
       [0.248, 0.397, 0.   , 0.068, 0.107, 0.141, 0.099, 0.568]])
```

After rescaling, you get the values between 0 and 1. By rescaling data, it confirms the use of neural networks, optimization algorithms as well as those which have distance measures such as the k-nearest neighbors.

2. Normalizing Data

In the following task, you rescale every observation to a specific length of 1. For this case, you use the Normalizer class. Here is an example:

```
>>> from sklearn.preprocessing import Normalizer
>>> scaler=Normalizer().fit(x)
>>> normalizedX=scaler.transform(x)
>>> normalizedX[0:5,:]
```

```
>>> normalizedX[0:5,:]
array([[2.024e-01, 1.914e-02, 0.000e+00, 5.196e-02, 2.079e-03, 3.008e-01,
        9.299e-01, 2.729e-02],
       [1.083e-01, 1.222e-02, 0.000e+00, 3.611e-02, 1.361e-03, 3.472e-01,
        9.306e-01, 1.385e-02],
       [1.377e-01, 1.342e-02, 7.061e-04, 4.060e-02, 1.624e-03, 2.648e-01,
        9.533e-01, 1.760e-02],
       [1.767e-01, 4.416e-03, 8.833e-03, 2.997e-02, 1.183e-03, 2.681e-01,
        9.464e-01, 1.574e-02],
       [2.024e-01, 1.914e-02, 0.000e+00, 5.196e-02, 2.079e-03, 3.008e-01,
        9.299e-01, 2.729e-02]])
```

3. Binarizing Data

If you use the binary threshold, it is possible to change the data and make the value above it to be 1 while those that are equal to or fall below it, 0. For this task, you use the Binarized class.

```
>>> from sklearn.preprocessing import Binarizer
>>> binarizer=Binarizer(threshold=0.0).fit(x)
>>> binaryX=binarizer.transform(x)
>>> binaryX[0:5,:]
```

```
>>> binaryX[0:5,:]
array([[1., 1., 0., 1., 1., 1., 1., 1.],
       [1., 1., 0., 1., 1., 1., 1., 1.],
       [1., 1., 1., 1., 1., 1., 1., 1.],
       [1., 1., 1., 1., 1., 1., 1., 1.],
       [1., 1., 0., 1., 1., 1., 1., 1.]])
```

As you can see, the python code will label 0 overall values equal to or less than 0, and label 1 over the rest.

4. Mean Removal

This is where you remove mean from each property to center it on zero.

5. One Hot Encoding

When you deal with a few and scattered numerical values, you might need to store them before you can carry out the One Hot Encoding. For the k-distinct values, you can change the feature into a k-dimensional vector that has a single value of 1 and 0 for the remaining values.

```
>>> from sklearn.preprocessing import OneHotEncoder
>>> encoder=OneHotEncoder()
>>> encoder.fit([[0,1,6,2],
[1,5,3,5],
[2,4,2,7],
[1,0,4,2]
])
```

6. Label Encoding

Sometimes labels can be words or numbers. If you want to label the training data, you need to use words to increase its readability. Label encoding changes word labels into numbers to allow algorithms to operate on them. Here's an example:

```
>>> from sklearn.preprocessing import LabelEncoder
>>> label_encoder=LabelEncoder()
>>> input_classes=['Havells','Philips','Syska','Eveready','Lloyd']
>>> label_encoder.fit(input_classes)
```

Chapter 4

Regression

Linear regression

Linear regression is one of the most popular types of predictive analysis. Linear regression involves the following two things:

1. Do the predictor variables forecast the results of an outcome variable accurately?

2. Which particular variable are key predictors of the final variable, and in what standard does it impact the outcome variable?

Naming variables

The regression's dependent variable has many different names. Some names include outcome variable, criterion variable, and many others. The independent variable can be called exogenous variable or repressors.

Functions of the regression analysis

1. Trend Forecasting

2. Determine the strength of predictors

3. Predict an effect

Breaking down regression

There are two basic states of regression-linear and multiple regression. Although there are different methods for complex data and analysis. Linear regression contains an independent variable to help forecast the outcome of a dependent variable. On the other hand, multiple regression has two or more independent variables to assist in predicting a result.

Regression is very useful to financial and investment institutions because it is used to predict the sales of a particular product or company based on the previous sales and GDP growth among many other factors. The capital pricing model is one of the most common regression models applied in the finance. The example below describes formulae used in the linear and multiple regression.

```
Linear Regression: Y = a + bX + u
Multiple Regression: Y = a + b1X1 + b2X2 + b3X3 + ... + btXt + u
In this case:
Y = variable which you want to predict (dependent variable)
X = variable which you are using to predict Y (independent variable)
a = the intercept
b = the slope
u = regression residual
```

Choosing the best regression model

Selecting the right linear regression model can be very hard and confusing. Trying to model it with a sample data cannot make it easier. This section reviews some of the most popular statistical methods which one can use to choose models, challenges that you might come across, and lists some practical advice to use to select the correct regression model.

It always begins with a researcher who would like to expand the relationship between the response variable and predictors. The research team that is accorded with the responsibility to perform investigation essentially measures a lot of variables but only has a few in the model. The analysts will make efforts to reduce the variables that are different and apply the ones which have an accurate relationship. As time moves on, the analysts continue to add more models.

Statistical methods to use to find the best regression model
If you want a great model in regression, then it is important to take into consideration the type of variables which you want to test as well as other variables which can affect the response.

Modified R-squared and Predicted R-squared.
Your model should have a higher modified and predicted R-squared values. The statistics are shown below help eliminate critical issues which revolve around R-squared.

- The adjusted R squared increases once a new term improves the model.

- Predicted R-squared belongs to the cross-validation that helps define the manner in which your model can generalize remaining data sets.

P-values for the Predictors
When it comes to regression, a low value of P denotes statistically significant terms. The term "Reducing the model" refers to the process of factoring in all candidate predictors contained in a model.

Stepwise regression
This is an automated technique which can select important predictors found in the exploratory stages of creating a model.

Real World Challenges

There are different statistical approaches for choosing the best model. However, complications still exist.

• The best model happens when the variables are measured by the study.

• The sample data could be unusual because of the type of data collection method. A false positive and false negative process happens when you handle samples.

• If you deal with enough models, you'll get variables that are significant but only correlated by chance.

• P-values can be different depending on the specific terms found in the model.

• Studies have discovered that the best subset regression and stepwise regression can't select the correct model.

Finding the correct Regression Model

Theory

Perform research done by other experts and reference it into your model. It is important that before you start regression analysis, you should develop ideas about the most significant variables. Developing something based on outcome from other people eases the process of collecting data.

Complexity

You may think that complex problems need a complex model. Well, that is not the case because studies show that even a simple model can provide an accurate prediction. Once there is a model with the same explanatory potential, the simplest model is likely to be a perfect choice. You just need to start with a simple model as you slowly advance the complexity of the model.

How to calculate the accuracy of the predictive model

There are different ways in which you can compute the accuracy of your model. Some of these methods include:

1. You divide the dataset into a test and training data set. Next, build the model based on the training set and apply the test set as a holdout sample to measure your trained model with the test data. The next thing to do is to compare the predicted values using actual values by computing the error by using measures like the "Mean Absolute Percent Error" (MAPE). If your MAPE is less than 10%, then you have a great model.

2. Another method is to calculate the "Confusion Matrix" to the computer False Positive Rate and False Negative Rate. These measures will allow a person to choose whether to accept the model or not. If you consider the cost of the errors, it becomes a critical stage of your decision whether to reject or accept the model.

3. Computing Receiver Operating Characteristic Curve (ROC) or the Lift Chart or Area under the curve (AUC) are other methods that you can use to decide on whether to reject or accept a model.

Chapter 5

Classification

Classification refers to the process of predicting the class of a particular data point. Classes are referred to as labels, targets, or categories. Classification predictive modeling is the procedure of estimating a mapping function (f) from input variables (X) to discrete output variables (y).

Let's take the example of spam detection in email service providers which can be selected as a classification challenge. This is an example of a binary classification

because there are just 2 classes: a spam and not a spam. A classifier takes advantage of training data to understand the way a specific input of variables is associated with a particular class. In the following example, known spam and non-spam emails should be used as the training data. When the classifier is accurately trained, you can use it to detect unknown email.

Classification is a field of supervised learning where targets come with the input data. There are many areas in real life where classification is applied. Some of these areas include medical diagnosis, credit approval, target marketing, and many more.

The classification has two types of learners.

1. Lazy learners

Lazy learners hold training data and wait till the time when a testing data arrives. Once the data arrives, classification is performed depending on the common data found in the training data. When you compare it to eager learners, lazy learners have a minimum time of training. However, more time is required in prediction. An example includes k-nearest neighbor and case-based reasoning which we shall look later in the chapter.

2. Eager learners

With eager learners, the classification model is created with respect to the type of training data before getting data for classification. It should be able to dedicate a single hypothesis that handles the whole instance space. Because of the construction of the model, eager learners will consume more training time and minimum time during prediction. Example of eager learners includes Artificial Neural Networks, Naive Bayes and Decision Tree.

Classification Algorithms

There are many different kinds of classification algorithms developed, however, it is hard to pick on one which is better than the other. This is because of a few factors such as the application and nature of the existing data set. For instance, if you have linearly separable classes, the linear classifiers such as Logistic regression, Fisher's linear discriminant can execute complex models.

Decision Tree

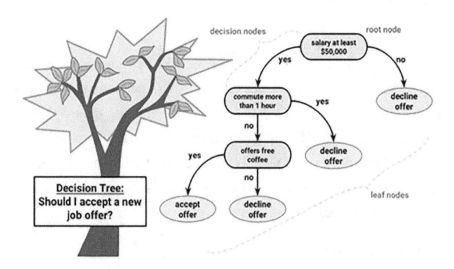

A decision tree creates regression models and classification models just like a tree structure. This tree works with the same concept as the if-then rule set that is mutually exclusive and exhaustive for classification. Rules are learned sequentially by applying the training data one at a time. Every time a rule is learned, the tuples which the rules handles are deleted. This process is repeated on the training set until a meeting termination condition is attained.

The tree is built through a technique called top-down recursive divide-and-conquer manner. All the features must be categorical. Nonetheless, they need to be discretized in advance. With a decision tree, it is very easy for overfitting to take place. Overfitting will produce many branches which may indicate problems of noise and outliers. In an overfitted model, the performance is very poor on the unseen data although it provides the correct performance on training data.

However, this is can be avoided by applying pre-pruning. Pre-pruning shall stop the tree construction early or post-pruning which eliminates branches from a complete tree.

Pros of Decision trees

1. Transparency

This is one of the most important advantages of the decision tree model. Unlike other models of the decision tree, the decision tree reveals all possible alternatives and traces each alternative to the end in a single view. This makes it easy to compare the different alternatives. The application of different nodes to represent user-defined decisions increases transparency in decision making.

2. Specificity

Another major advantage of the decision tree in the analysis is the ability to allocate a given value to a problem and outcomes of every decision. This is important because it helps minimize vagueness in the decision making. Every possible case from a decision tree discovers a representation using a clear fork and node. This allows one to see all solutions in a clear view. The inclusion of monetary values to decision tree reveals the costs and benefits of taking a different course of action.

3. Ease of use

The decision tree has a graphical representation of the problem and different alternatives in an easy and simple way to help any person understand without asking for an explanation.

4. Comprehensive nature

The decision tree is one of the best predictive models because it has a comprehensive analysis of the results of every possible decision. That can include what the decision leads to, if it finishes in uncertainty or whether it results to new issues which the process may require repetition.

5. They implicitly perform feature selection.

6. Decision trees can deal with categorical and numerical data.

7. Users have little to do with data preparation.

8. Nonlinear relationships between parameters cannot affect the performance.

Disadvantages of Decision trees
1. There are times when decision trees can be unstable because of the little variations in the data that may lead to a totally different tree generated.

2. The greedy algorithm cannot prove that it will return a universally optimal decision tree. This can be solved by training multiple trees where the samples and features have been randomly sampled with replacement.

3. Learners of the decision tree can build advanced trees that don't generalize the data.

4. Decision tree learners can be biased if there are classes which dominate.

For that reason, it is advised to balance the data set before fitting with the decision tree.

K-Nearest Neighbor (KNN)

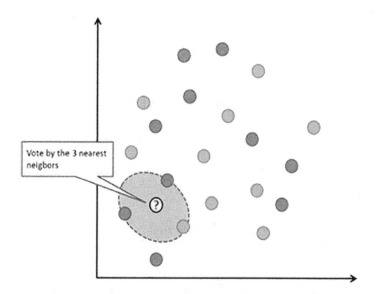

The k-nearest Neighbor belongs to the lazy learning algorithm which holds all instances that match to training data points in n-dimensional space. In case there is an unknown discrete data, it has to make an analysis of the nearest k number of instances saved and display the most popular class as the prediction. For the real-valued data, it has to return the mean of k-nearest neighbors.

In the case of the distance-weighted nearest neighbor algorithm, it measures the weight of every k-nearest neighbor based on their distance by applying the query below.

$$w \equiv \frac{1}{d(x_q, x_i)^2}$$

Distance calculating query

Typically, KNN is very strong to noisy data because it averages the k-nearest neighbors.

Pros of KNN

- A simple algorithm to explain and understand

- It doesn't make any assumptions about data.

- It has a higher accuracy that is not comparable to other better-supervised learning models.

- It is versatile for classification and regression.

Cons of KNN

- Calls for a higher memory requirement

- It is computationally expensive since the algorithm has all the training data.

Quick features of KNN

- This algorithm holds the whole training dataset that uses as a representation.

- It doesn't learn any model.

- It performs timely predictions by calculating the similarity between sample input and instance training.

Where Can You Apply K-means

K-means is used with data that is numeric, continuous and has a small dimension. Imagine an instance where you would like to group similar items from a randomly spread collection of things such as k-means. This list has a few interesting areas where you can apply K-means

1. Classification of documents

Clustering of documents in numerous categories depends on topics, tags, and the content of the document. This is a normal classification problem and k-means is a great algorithm for this function. The original document processing is important when you want to replace every document as a sector and applies the frequency term to use terms which classify the document. The vectors of the document have to be clustered so that they can select similarity in document groups.

2. Delivery store Optimization

If you want to improve the process of delivery, you'll need to enhance it by applying drones and integrating k-means algorithm to determine the optimal number of launch locations and a genetic algorithm to compute the route of the truck.

3. Fantasy League Stat Analysis

To analyze the stats of a player is one of the most critical features of the sporting world. With the rapid rise of competition, machine learning has an important function to offer here. As a great exercise, if you want to build a fantasy draft team and select similar players, k-means is a great option.

4. Rideshare Data analysis

Information about Uber is available to the public. This dataset has an extensive size of valuable data about transit time, traffic, peak pickup localities, and many more. If you analyze this particular data, you will get insight into the urban traffic patterns and help plan for the cities in the future.

5. Cyber-profiling criminals

This is the process of gathering data from people and groups to select important links. The concept behind cyber-profiling is extracted from criminal histories that provide information about investigation division to help categorize criminals present at the crime.

6. Automatic clustering of IT Alerts

Extensive enterprise in IT infrastructure technology like network generates huge volumes of alert messages. Since alert messages refer to operational issues, it has to be manually screened for categorization. Data clustering can help provide insight into alert categories and the mean time to repair and support predictions.

7. Identify crime localities

Since data associated to crime is present in specific city localities, the type of crime, the area of the crime, and the relation between the two can provide quality insight into the most crime-prone areas in the city or a locality.

Artificial Neural Network

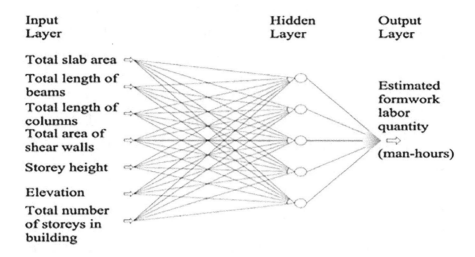

Artificial Neural Network describes a set of connected input/output where every connection is linked to a particular weight. In the learning phase, the network adjusts the weights so that it can predict the right class label of input tuples.

There are a lot of network architectures present now. Some of them include the Feed-forward, Recurrent, Convolutional, etc. The correct architecture depends on the model application. In most cases, the feed-forward models provide a reasonably accurate result and mostly for image processing applications.

There can be many hidden layers in a model based on the complexity of the function that is to be wrapped by the model. If you have a lot of hidden layers, it will facilitate the modeling of complex relationships like deep neural networks.

However, the presence of many hidden layers increases the time it takes to train and adjust weights. Another drawback is the poor interpretability when compared to other models such as Decision Trees.

Despite this, ANN has performed well in the majority of the real-world applications. It has an intensive persistence to noisy data and can categorize untrained patterns. Generally, ANN works better with continuous-valued inputs and outputs.

Pros of ANN

•   It stores information in the whole network. For example, traditional programming information is kept in the whole network, and not in a database. This means that loss of certain information in a given place does not stop the network functions.

•   It has fault tolerance. The destruction of one or more cells of ANN doesn't affect it from producing input. Therefore, this specific feature causes the network to be fault tolerant.

•   It can work with incomplete knowledge. Once the ANN training is over, the data can produce output using incomplete information. The loss of performance, in this case, will depend on the missing information.

•   ANN has the ability to make machine learning.

•   It has a parallel processing capability. The ANN neural networks feature a numerical strength that does more than one job at the same time.

Disadvantages of ANN

•   It depends on the hardware. ANN need processors which contain parallel processing power based on their structure. For this case, the realization of the device is dependent.

•   The determination of the correct network structure. Often, there is no fixed rule to use to determine the structure of artificial neural networks. The right network structure is attained through trial and error.

•   The duration of the network is not known. The network is limited to a particular value of the error on the sample means which the training is completed. This value does not generate an optimum result.

•   There are unexplained characteristics of the network. It is one of the major problems of ANN. If an ANN generates a probing solution, it doesn't show any hint. This always reduces trust in the network.

Naïve Bayes

The Naïve Bayes algorithm is a probabilistic classifier which was driven by the Bayes theorem. This is based on a simple assumption where attributes are conditionally independent.

$$P(\mathbf{X} \mid C_i) = \prod_{k=1}^{n} P(x_k \mid C_i) = P(x_1 \mid C_i) \times P(x_2 \mid C_i) \times ... \times P(x_n \mid C_i)$$

The classification works by extracting the maximum posterior that is the maximal $P(C_i|\mathbf{X})$ with the above-stated assumption working. This assumption always reduces the computational cost by measuring the computational cost. Although the assumption fails many times because the properties are dependent. Despite this, the Naïve Bayes has continued to work so well.

This is a simple algorithm to implement and improve outcomes that have been generated in most instances. It is possible for it to be scaled into massive datasets because it assumes a linear time.

Pros of Naïve Bayes

- It is simple and easy to implement.

- It requires minimal training data.

- It handles continuous and discrete data.

- It can develop probabilistic predictions.

- It is highly scalable.

Cons of Naïve Bayes

- It makes a robust assumption regarding the shape of the data distribution.

- There are challenges related to data scarcity.

- The issue of continuous features that requires a binning procedure to make them discrete.

Classification Accuracy Metrics
This refers to the ratio of the number of correct predictions to the general number of input samples.

$$Accuracy = \frac{Number\ of\ Correct\ predictions}{Total\ number\ of\ predictions\ made}$$

It works better when the number of samples which belong to each class is equal. Classification accuracy is the best but provides a false notion of attaining high accuracy.

The major problem emerges when the cost of misclassification of minor class samples is high. If you are to handle a rare but dangerous disease, the cost of not diagnosing the disease of a sick individual is very high compared to the cost of testing a healthy person.

Logarithmic Loss

This operates well for multi-class classification. When you work with Log Loss, the classifier has to allocate probability for every class. For example, if you have N samples of M classes, you can compute the Log Loss as follows:

$$LogarithmicLoss = \frac{-1}{N}\sum_{i=1}^{N}\sum_{j=1}^{M} y_{ij} * \log(p_{ij})$$

where,

y_ij, indicates whether sample i belongs to class j or not

p_ij, indicates the probability of sample i belonging to class j

Confusion Matrix

Confusion matrix as the name suggests creates a matrix as the output and explains the complete performance of a model.

Suppose you have a binary classification problem. Then there are some samples which belong to two classes: YES or NO. Additionally, you have your own classifier that can predict a class for a particular input sample. If the following model is tested on 165 samples, the following result is obtained.

n=165	Predicted: NO	Predicted: YES
Actual: NO	50	10
Actual: YES	5	100

There are four major terms:

1.   True Positives. This is where our prediction was YES and final outcome YES.

2.   True Negatives. This is where our prediction was NO and final outcome NO.

3.   False Positives. In this case, the prediction was YES but the final outcome was NO.

4.   False Negatives. In this scenario, the prediction was NO but the final outcome was YES.

Area Under the Curve

This is one of the most widely applied metrics for evaluation. It is applied in binary application problems.

Other metrics include:

- Mean absolute error

- Mean squared error

Chapter 6

Clustering

Clustering is the process of gathering entities with similar characteristics together. This technique belongs to unsupervised machine learning whose target is to identify similarities in the data point and group the same data points together.

Why apply Clustering?

By grouping similar entities in one place allows one to identify the attributes of different groups. In other words, this generates insight into the underlying patterns of various groups. There are countless application areas of grouping unlabeled data.

For example, it is possible to select different groups of customers and market every group differently to take advantage of the revenue. Another example may include grouping documents together that belong to similar topics. Additionally, clustering is used to reduce the dimensionality of the data when you handle various copious variables.

3 Main Types of Clustering

Partitioned-based clustering

The phrase cluster doesn't have an accurate definition. A cluster describes a set of points whereby any point in the cluster is close to any other point in the cluster than a point absent in the cluster. Sometimes, a threshold is used to define all points in a cluster close to one another.

A partitioning method will first create an original set of K-partitions where k- parameter is the number of partitions to construct. Next, it applies an iterative relocation approach which tries to enhance the partitioning by shifting objects from one group to another. These clustering techniques help generate a one-level partitioning of data points. There are various partitioning-based clustering like K-means, fuzzy C-, means, and K-medoids. This section will look at K-mean clustering.

K-mean Clustering

1. It begins with K as the input. This refers to the number of clusters that you want to find. Assign K-centroids in random positions in your space.

2. Now, if you use the Euclidean distance between data points and centroids, allocate each data point to the cluster close to it.

3. Re-compute the cluster centers as a mean of data points allocated to it.

4. Repeat 2 and 3 till there are no more changes to happen.

You might be wondering how you can select the value of K.

One method is the "Elbow" that is used to define an optimal number of clusters. In this case, you'll run the range of K values and plot the "percentage of variance explained," on Y-axis and "K" on the "X" axis.

In the diagram below, more clusters have been added after 3. These additional clusters affect the display of the model. The first cluster adds more information, and at a certain point, the marginal gain will start to drop.

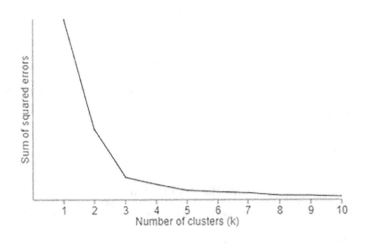

Hierarchical clustering

With the Hierarchical clustering, it begins by assigning all data points to belong to its own cluster. Just as the name implies, it creates the hierarchy and in the next step, it integrates the two closest data point and combines it together into a single cluster.

1. Allocate every data point to its cluster.

2. Determine the closest pair of the cluster by applying the Euclidean distance and combine it into a single cluster.

3. Determine the distance between two nearest clusters and integrate them until when all items are grouped into a single cluster.

In the next method, you can choose the best number of clusters by identifying which vertical lines are cut by a horizontal line without affecting a cluster and deals with the maximum distance.

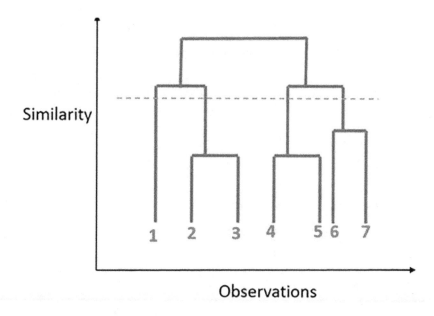

Similarity

Observations

Density Based Clustering

The basic concept underlying density-based clustering technique is extracted from a human perception clustering method. For example, if you look at the images below, you should be able to see four clusters plus different points of noise.

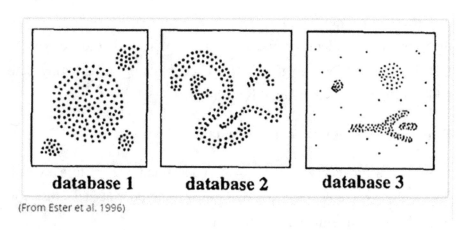

database 1   database 2   database 3

(From Ester et al. 1996)

As shown in the above image, the clusters are dense regions in the data space that are delineated by regions of a lower density point. In short,

63

the density of points in a cluster is somehow higher compared to the density of points located outside the cluster.

The density-based clustering algorithm depends on an intuitive perception of "clusters" and "noise". The point is that for every cluster, the neighborhood of a particular radius should have at least a minimum.

The most important parameters are needed for DBSCAN include ("eps") and minimum points ("MinPts"). The parameter eps determine the radius of the neighborhood around close to a point x. The parameter MinPts describes the minimum number of neighbors in the "eps" radius.

Any point x that exists in the dataset that has a count higher than or equal to MinPts is identified as a core point.

Customer Segmentation with Cluster analysis

The customer base of a company can have thousands, if not millions, of different unique persons. Marketing, to most of these people, presents a big problem because if you attempt to market to everybody, the message can be ambiguous. However, building a marketing plan which attracts every individual is not normal.

Why customer segments are important

Customer segments will make you understand the patterns which distinguish your customers. Below are some important ideas that you can achieve with segmentation analysis.

- Enhanced understanding of the customer needs and wants. This can lead to improved sales and customer satisfaction.

- Create products that appeal to different customer segments.

- Companies cannot fulfill all possible customers all the time. By applying segmentation procedure, companies have the ability to concentrate on fulfilling those segments which they examine to be the best attractions for their products.

- Build loyal relationships.

While you can analyze your own customer base, soon it shall be clear that there are different groups that have customized requirements. This allows you to build a deeper understanding of your customers and find out what makes them tick.

It is no gem that a customer is always more profitable compared to others. However, to be profitable, businesses should have a better understanding of the way profitability relates to customer segmentation. Discovering the difference between customers will permit one to personalize your method to the desires of the customer segments.

Customer segmentation describes the practice of categorizing a customer base into different groups of individuals similar in a given way. Customer segments are often determined based on similarities such as personal characteristics, behaviors, and preferences. By understanding your customers and their differences, it becomes one of the most important stages of measuring the customers' relationship.

How to segment
Segmentation doesn't need to be very complex. For a small organization or company, it can be about discovering that you have

two or three unique customer types who have different needs. Some popular methods used to segment customers consist of:

- Demographic

- Behavioral

- Psychographic

- Geographic

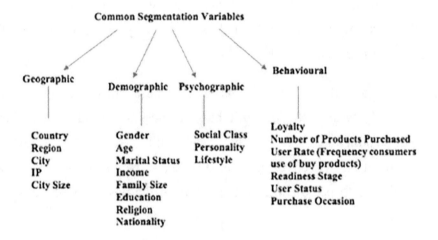

There are different ways which you can apply when it comes to segmentation of a market. One of the methods that are accurate and statistically valid is the application of cluster analysis.

Chapter 7

Recommender Systems

Most e-commerce and retail companies are taking advantage of the massive potential of data to boost sales by implementing a Recommender system on their particular websites.

These systems focus on suggesting to the user's items that they may like or have interest in.

The data needed for recommendation engines comes from explicit user ratings to watch a movie or listen to a song from implicit search engine purchase histories and queries. Sites such as YouTube, Spotify, and Netflix have data to use to recommend playlists.

Pros of using recommendation systems
Companies which apply the Recommender system concentrate on raising the sales due to the personalized offers and improved customer experience.

Recommendations usually increase searches and make it easy for users to access content which they are interested in, and surprise them with offers that they have never searched before.

What is interesting is that companies can now gain and retain customers by sending out email links to new offers that fulfill the interests of their profiles.

By creating an added advantage to users through suggesting products and systems, it creates a great feeling among buyers. This is a great thing because it will allow companies to stay ahead of their competitors.

Types of Recommender Systems

Recommender systems operate with two types of information:

- User-item interactions

- Characteristic information

This helps us reach the first classification of recommender systems. This includes a content-based system that has a characteristic information and collaborative filtering which depends on user-item interactions. The hybrid systems shall combine both information with the goal to avoid problems generated when you work with only one specific type.

Content-based Systems

Content-based systems are built from the idea of applying the content of each product for purposes of recommendation. Below are some pros and cons of the content-based recommender system.

Pros

- It is simple to create a more transparent system. You use the same content to describe the recommendations.

- Content representations are different and they open up the options to apply unique approaches like text processing techniques, inferences, and semantic information.

- In case of items have enough descriptions, there is no need for the "new item problem".

Cons

- The content-based RecSys seem to over-specialize. They will suggest items similar to that which is already consumed, with a notion to create a "filter bubble".

Another issue is that new users don't have a defined profile not unless they are explicitly requested for information. Despite this, it is very simple to add new items to the system. You simply require to allocate them a group based on their features.

Three principal components

- A content Analyzer-This classifies items using a given type of representation.

- A profile Learner-It creates a profile which represents every user's preference.

- A filtering Component-It accepts all the inputs and creates a list of recommendations for every user.

How content is represented

The content of a particular item is abstract and provides more options. You can use many different variables. For instance, for a book, you can include the genre, author, the text of the book and many other factors.

Once you know which content you will factor. You need to convert all the data into a vector space model, which is an algebraic representation of text documents.

You perform this using a Bag of Words model which represents documents disregarding the sequence of words. In this particular model, every document appears like a bag with some words. Therefore, this method will permit word modeling with respect to dictionaries, where every bag has some words from the dictionary.

An exact implementation of a Bag of Words is the TF-IDF representation. In full, TF stands for Term Frequency and IDF stands for Inverse Document Frequency. This particular model combines the significance of the word in the document with the significance of the world in the corpus.

This was just a general aspect of Content-based recommendation engines. It is important to recognize that a Bag of Words representation doesn't factor in the context of words. If it is necessary to include that, Semantic Content Representation becomes useful. Below are two options that one has, just in case you want to know more about it.

Option 1: Explicit Semantic Representation

- Wordnet

- ConceptNet

- Ontologies for Semantic Representation

Option 2: Infer Semantic Representation

- Latent Dirichlet Allocation

- Latent Semantic Indexing

Collaborative filtering systems

These types of recommendation engine implement user interactions to evaluate items of interest. You can visualize the set of interactions using a matrix where every entry (I, j) represents the interactions between user i and item j. One way of looking at collaborative filtering is to look at it as a generalization of regression and classification. In the following case, you aim to predict a variable directly which depends on other variables in the collaborative filtering.

Visualizing a problem as a matrix allows us not only to predict the values of a unique column but also help us predict the values of any entry.

Techniques to apply in collaborative filtering
There is a lot of research that has been done on collaborative filtering, and most common techniques depend on low-dimensional factor models that depend on matrix factorization. The CF techniques are divided into 2 types:

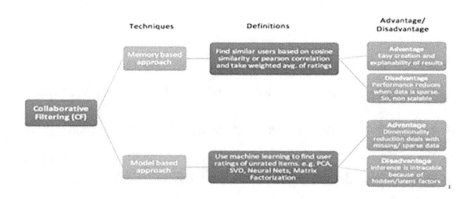

Types of collaborative filtering approaches. Reference: Wikipedia

Below is a brief discussion of some of these techniques

1. Memory-based technique
This approach can further be divided into two sections: User-item filtering and item-item filtering. The user-item filtering selects a given

71

user, searches for users that are similar to the user depending on the similarity of the ratings, and suggest items that the same users recommended. On the other hand, item-item filtering will identify an item, search users who liked an item and look for other products that the same users liked. In other words, this approach takes items and displays the items as recommendations.

The major difference of memory-based technique from the model-based techniques is that no parameter is learned using gradient descent.

2. Model-based approach
In this particular approach, CF models are created using machine learning algorithms to predict the ratings of items unrelated to the user.

Content-Based Filtering

This system will suggest an item to users depending on their past history.

The greatest advantage of content-based filtering is that it can start to suggest items immediately information related to items is available.

A content-based system will work with information which the user provides, this can be explicitly or implicitly. Depending on data, a user profile is created that provides a lot of inputs or takes actions about recommendations.

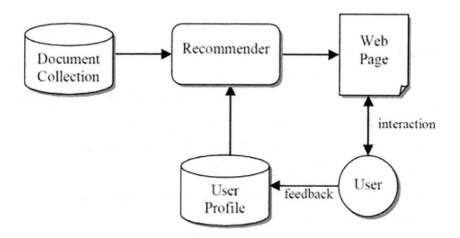

Conclusion

With some knowledge of basic Python, machine learning skills, and Python libraries, you are now set to launch your first machine learning project with Python. Consider learning the open-source Python libraries. The scientific Python libraries will help you complete easy machine learning tasks. However, the choice of some of these libraries can be completely subjective and highly debatable by many people in the industry.

All in all, we recommend you to start by exploring Scikit-learn library. Make sure you are familiar with its concepts and how to use it. Once you are done with it, you can dive deep into advanced machine learning topics such as complex data transformation and vector machines.

Just like how a child learns how to walk is the same with learning Machine Learning with Python. You need to practice many times before you can become better. Practice different algorithms and use different datasets to improve your knowledge and overall problem-solving skills.

www.ingramcontent.com/pod-product-compliance
Lightning Source LLC
LaVergne TN
LVHW051748050326
832903LV00029B/2785